WILD WATER CANOEING

On the Brathay

WILD WATER CANOEING

FRED BARLOW

CICERONE PRESS

MILNTHORPE CUMBRIA ENGLAND

© Fred Barlow 1989
ISBN 1 85284 031 5

ACKNOWLEDGEMENTS

To the many people who have helped in the preparation of this book:

Bryan Mitchinson who who took many of the photographs; Frank Goodman of Valley Canoe Products for his help and advice on the proposed British Standard for white-water canoes; the many people who have instructed me on innumerable occasions and courses, in particular Charlie Wilson; the staff of the Mountain Centre for the original typing of the script; Wal Greenhalgh for the correcting of many errors, proof-reading of the script and the final presentation.

 I dedicate this book to Joan Barlow, who has cheerfully accepted accompanying me on many occasions, and whose advice I am grateful to have, and also for the help and freely given advice of my daughter Mary Sargeant.

Fred Barlow, 1989

CONTENTS

ROB ROY CANOE

Chapter 1
History of Canoes, and types of craft

All types of canoe sport have developed rapidly in recent years. The earliest type of canoe, as we know it, was the sea-going Eskimo kayak, built from laths held in shape by frames, and then covered with skin. The interesting feature about these boats is that they were made from materials which were readily available in the north. The frames were made from bones of animals slaughtered for food, and stringers were made from drift-wood held together by leather thongs. The Eskimo kayak developed into a highly efficient machine and was a very stable boat, now copied in glass fibre for sea-going canoes.

A book on the Rob Roy canoe published early in the 20th century captured the imagination of a number of designers, who produced plans of boats using plywood frames and stringers of pine and covered in canvas. These designs were very light in weight; some were modified to fold, to be easily transported by train for expeditions to remote waters.

A fault in the design of frame and stringer canoes was that the water pressure gave a corrugated effect to the canvas, making the boat difficult to turn, and the lightness of the whole construction made damage in rocky rivers inevitable.

The introduction of glass-fibre reinforced plastics influenced canoe construction. Moulds were taken off the canvas canoe, easing out the corrugation, to produce a rounded or elliptical cross-section for the new designs. From these moulds many canoes could be produced of identical design, with a smooth surface presented to the water. Canoeists eagerly modified the boat design, to produce boats faster and more manoeuvrability in slalom conditions. Some were of very extreme design suitable only for slalom or down-river competition. The novice should take advice before purchasing his first boat.

Glass-fibre reinforced plastics produce an extremely strong boat which can be bounced off rocks with little damage or, if damage occurs, can easily be repaired. This results in canoeists looking for

7

more and more rapid rivers, with sometimes a conflict between the canoeist and sports fishermen.

The sea offers a suitable alternative to river canoeing, particularly at the tide's edge where breaking waves give scope for practising one's wild water techniques. This type of canoeing has developed into a sport known as surfing, in which slalom-type boats are raced in competition down the flanks of waves, giving exciting sport. Designers have developed boats without cockpits especially for this sport. Canoeists also venture on the sea with extended coastal trips in mind. Slalom-type canoes are often used but designs copied from the Eskimo kayak are more suitable, with a hard-chine hull and raised bow to cut through the waves. Often the boats are five metres long with sealed bulkheads, making them very suitable for extended trips carrying camping gear. Kayaks of this type can often be seen off the west coast of Scotland, where trips in sea-lochs and round islands offer magnificent scenery and a challenge.

White Water Canoeing in a PolyethyleneBoat
Photo — Brian Mitchinson

The polyethylene canoe has now arrived. Initially produced in unsuitable material of a floppy nature, it would flatten when resting on a surface and would fold up on its occupants if stressed. These problems have now been resolved by the use of a stronger plastic and improved design round the cockpit area, and polyethylene boats are now sold in either cross-linked or linear plastic. To produce these boats requires an expensive mould and a machine to inject the plastic. Production runs must be in the thousands, and innovation is not possible. Bows and sterns must be rounded. Many boats are produced under four metres long, which are described as fun-boats and under present slalom rules are not allowed in competition.

These very tough boats can be canoed in boulder-choked rivers, thus extending canoe sport further upstream. However, the cockpit area is still a weakness, and it is possible under extreme circumstances for the boat to fold, trapping the occupant in the canoe. The solution appears to be a pod containing the seat and foot-rest which could be released in this hazardous situation.

Types of Craft

When buying a canoe, many people little realise that there is a variety of designs and that the craft they fancy may not be suitable for the purpose for which they intend to use it. If you visit a boating centre, the selection could well be one canoe amid a collection of sailing boats and dinghies. It is difficult to find comprehensive stockists of canoes, not to mention staff who are familiar with all aspects of the sport.

The typical canoe available from a stockist would be a touring canoe with a flat keel line and a beam of about 24 inches. This boat is capable of carrying a heavy load, would run straight in any water, and would be very difficult to tip over; but it would be a rather uninteresting boat to paddle, most suitable for stretches of flat water and mature rivers. They can be purchased as either double- or single-seat canoes.

Sea Canoes or Kayaks

The sea canoe is a rather specialised type of canoe, again with a flat keel and a hard chine, V-shaped hull. The deck profile is designed to cut through waves, with an uplifted bow and stern, a V-shaped

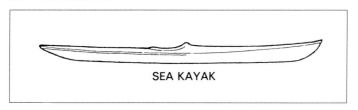

SEA KAYAK

foredeck to shed the water, and usually a flat rear deck. They lie low in the water to prevent windage (being blown off course by the wind), and the design, based on the Eskimo kayak, is very suitable for open stretches of water. Some have sealed buoyancy tanks with deck hatches.

Canadian Canoes

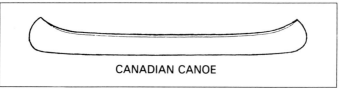

CANADIAN CANOE

These are of two types. The first is the traditional 'Red Indian' canoe, double or single, propelled with a single-bladed paddle with a specialist stroke known as the J-stroke. It is capable of carrying a ton of equipment and is ideal for camping. There is also a decked-over Canadian canoe, used exclusively for wild-water competition, which bears little resemblance to the traditional Canadian canoe but is propelled by the same method. It is constructed in aluminium, fibre-glass or polyethylene.

Racing Canoes

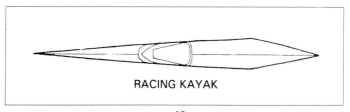

RACING KAYAK

Wild-water racing canoes are not suitable boats for a beginner. They are arrow-shaped in plan, with a straight keel, designed to make fast progress in heavy water.

Slalom Canoes

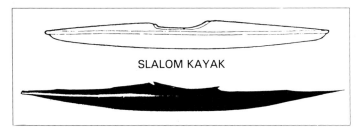

SLALOM KAYAK

The slalom canoe is a standard length (four metres) with a rockered keel which makes it highly manoeuvrable. There are many designs, the latest being very 'extreme', capable of dipping bow or stern into the water to avoid slalom gates. The hull of this canoe is either U-shaped or elliptical in section, making it easy to roll. It can be high- or low-volume; a low-volume boat is often described as a wet boat.

Mini-Canoes

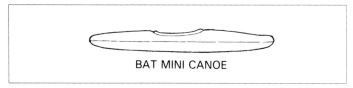

BAT MINI CANOE

There are a number of mini-canoes on the market which are ideal for carrying on the roof of a car, as they are only eight or ten feet long. These should be regarded as fun boats and are useful for learning techniques. This type of boat has been used on very rapid rivers when made of polyethylene and packed full of buoyancy.

Surf Boats

With the development of canoe surfing a number of designs of surf boat are being produced, specifically for the sole purpose of surf-

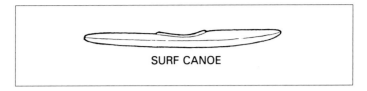

SURF CANOE

running; they may be with or without cockpits.

Double Canoes

People often ask canoe salesmen for a double canoe, but it is twice the price of a single and there are limits to the manoeuvres one is able to perform with the double. More enjoyment can be had initially from developing the skills of the sport in a single canoe.

Double canoes are often used in long-distance racing. (The 'Devizes to Westminster' is one such event.) The person sitting in the front seat of the canoe acts as pacemaker, dictating the strokes. The

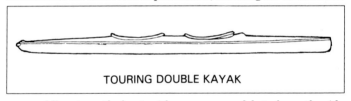

TOURING DOUBLE KAYAK

rear paddler steers the boat, with a more powerful stroke on the side needing correcting. When paddling into a cross wind, holding the paddle with a bigger lever on one side of the boat will give self-steerage. A rudder with lines into the cockpit also helps.

Choosing a Canoe

From this bewildering choice, the novice who wishes to develop his skill in the sport would be well advised to choose a slalom-type canoe with a V-shaped deck, while avoiding the extreme racing versions. Ensure that it has buoyancy; a vertical buoyancy block is useful and helps to support the deck as well. A foot-rest of the fail-safe type is most important. Canoeists' legs have been known to go past the foot-rest on hitting an obstacle in the water, and they have been trapped in the boat, unable to withdraw their feet. The fail-safe foot-rest acts rather like a latch and opens backwards, and is an essential feature.

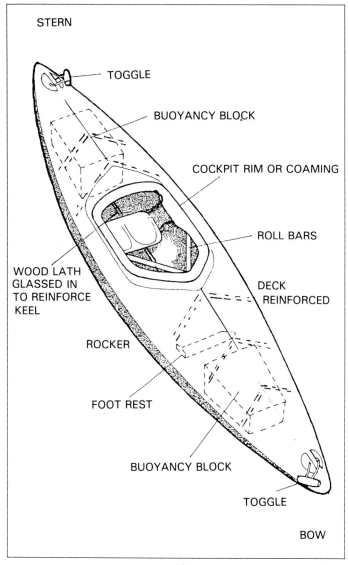

STERN

TOGGLE

BUOYANCY BLOCK

COCKPIT RIM OR COAMING

ROLL BARS

WOOD LATH
GLASSED IN
TO REINFORCE
KEEL

DECK
REINFORCED

ROCKER

FOOT REST

BUOYANCY BLOCK

TOGGLE

BOW

Look at the cockpit and try the seat, as some seat mouldings are rather uncomfortable to sit in for any length of time. Roll bars have some advantages, giving you a better grip in the boat with your thighs and also avoiding a sharp edge. Toggles should be fitted on bow and stern, for ease of carrying, and, more important, as something to grab when out of the canoe and in the water. An elastic-fitted spray deck, with a release tab, will prevent water entering the boat, and should be tight enough to maintain a good seal.

Don't buy your own canoe until you have some experience and have had the chance to try out a number of makes and types. Ask advice and chat to as many canoeists as you can. Quite often they will let you try out their own craft and experience the features it contains. Finally, go to a good, competent stockist, perhaps a BCU Instructor. Read the journals and study the advertisements. Take time to choose before you buy.

* * *

Proposed British Standard for Canoes Designed for White-Water Use

High-volume boats are recommended for white-water use but should be related to the canoeist's body weight.

The design should allow the canoeists to exit from the cockpit easily, with no obstruction or high back-straps in the rear of the boat, and the knees must be able to be easily lifted clear of the cockpit when rapid exit is necessary. The cockpit area must be sufficiently strong to resist bending or collapsing. End grabs should be strong enough to withstand a load of 500kg and should be positioned on the bow and stern to avoid snagging. Loops should be fastened in two holes more than four fingers' width apart. They and

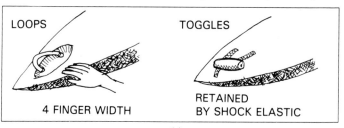

LOOPS   TOGGLES

4 FINGER WIDTH   RETAINED BY SHOCK ELASTIC

toggles should be designed so that the hand cannot be trapped if the canoe rolls over, and should be capable of taking a karabiner for rescue purposes. Deck-lines around the cockpit are thought to be dangerous and if fitted should only be single and pulled tight.

The foot-rest should be a shock-absorbing platform and should allow no possibility of the foot sliding past it, and should be designed to take a load of 500kg. Buoyancy should take up all unoccupied space and give resistance to folding of the boat. With buoyancy the boat floats higher in the water, and less water rolling around inside the canoe helps stability when swamped. Compartments filled with air are not considered a satisfactory method of providing buoyancy.

A safe boat will reduce accidents, but the skill of the paddler is the most important factor if the canoeist is to remain safe.

Chapter 2
Equipment

Paddles

The choice of paddle can be as bewildering as the choice of a canoe. Consideration must be given as to how the paddle is used, for not only is it a means of propelling the boat, but it also acts as a rudder to steer the canoe and a lever to support the canoeist. The traditional paddle, double-bladed, with a brass ferrule in the middle which allowed the paddle to be split into two and the blade to be feathered, has now been discarded in favour of a single-piece paddle.

The beginner would be advised to buy a paddle kit, which consists of an aluminium tube four feet in length, plastic covered for comfort and grip, and two flat blades. These are assembled feathered, at right angles to each other. From this initial paddle the canoeist can, with experience, progress to a more responsive paddle having discovered which way he rolls his wrist and his own particular preference for paddling.

Undoubtedly the best paddles are constructed of laminated wood, often several different types of timber being used in the laminations - spruce and ash for strength, beech or mahogany to protect from abrasion - and the blades tipped with metal for protection. These paddles have an oval grip and a curved blade; paddles of this type can be spliced to any length, and there is of course either a left-hand or a right-hand feather.

A modern paddle, being hand-made, is naturally expensive. Manufacturers have experimented with other materials, mainly carbon-fibre or glass-fibre for shafts and many forms of laminated plastic for blades, most of which have some technical disadvantage. Glass-fibre blades have been well tried; they need a supporting brace along their length and have usually only one smooth face, the reverse side being finished in glass cloth. Although hard-wearing, they have a disconcerting habit of flopping when under load. Other synthetic materials used for blades are normally rather heavy, although the glass-reinforced foamed polypropylene with a glass-

Corrected paddle for windage. Photo: Brian Mitchinson

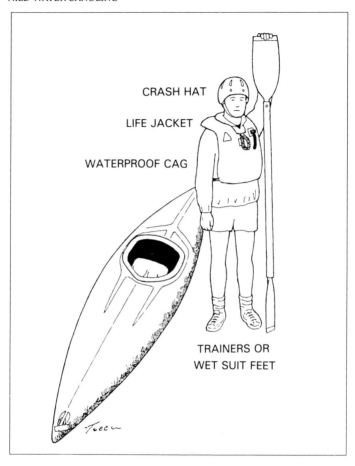

CRASH HAT

LIFE JACKET

WATERPROOF CAG

TRAINERS OR
WET SUIT FEET

fibre loom, handles similarly to a conventional wooden paddle.

Spraydecks

These have the purpose of keeping water out of the canoe, retaining heat inside the boat to keep the canoeist warm. In heavy water they must be burst-proof and of necessity must be a tight fit. They must release if the canoeist is forced out of the canoe. A strap must be

18

fitted around the deck in a position to be grabbed easily in an emergency, preferably sewn strongly on both sides; these are normally made out of nylon.

Neoprene decks are now favoured; it is a stretchy material, so that the canoeist can position himself in the cockpit to perform any manoeuvre required, and they are completely burst-proof.

Clothing

This is always a problem in water sports. Wet-suits have almost become standard equipment for an extended trip in the cooler seasons of the year, but they have a number of disadvantages for the canoeists. If dry, they tend to overheat the wearer when paddling, and restriction round the arms tends to make paddling a greater effort. When the suit becomes wet the water evaporating from it has a chilling effect. To avoid this problem a waterproof outer garment is necessary. Some canoeists feel that the ideal is a wet-suit bottom with a waterproof top; but this arrangement presents a hazard if the canoeist finds himself in the water, for the buoyancy of the wet-suit trousers will tend to invert him in the water.

A dry suit has therefore been developed for canoe sport. Worn over the top of a track suit and sealed at the ankles, wrist and neck, and loose-fitting around the body, it keeps canoeists dry. After exertion caused by hard paddling, the suit can become rather sticky inside. Heat loss from the extremities can be solved by wet-suit boots in which you can wade without getting your feet wet, and if the water comes over the top your feet will stay warm, though wet. Incidentally, Wellingtons should never be worn by canoeists as the possibility of getting your feet trapped is considerable, and this can be dangerous.

The greatest heat loss occurs around the head and neck. A woollen ski hat, pulled well down over your ears and worn under a crash hat, will keep you warm even though wet. Hands are a major problem. A satisfactory solution that I have discovered is a pair of silk inner gloves worn under domestic rubber gloves; this gives a satisfactory grip on the paddle and takes the chill from wind and water.

Crash hats are now preferred by most wild-water canoeists. Types developed for canoeing have holes in the shells to let water out. They must be well padded inside. The British Canoe Union has approved some designs.

Equipped Canoeist.   Photo: Brian Mitchinson

Life Jackets and Buoyancy Aids

Life jackets are essential for all water sports. The habit should be established of putting on a life jacket before getting into the boat, however shallow the water or short the journey. The British Canoe Union has approved British Standard No.3595 as the best proposition. Many canoeists prefer a buoyancy aid which gives a certain amount of body protection if you find yourself in a rapid river being pounded against rocks. The disadvantage of a buoyancy aid is that it is incapable of rolling the wearer on his back and keeping his face above water, should he become unconscious.

Good equipment is expensive, as it has to stand up to a lot of hard wear and give protection from the elements. This is not an area where you can afford to skimp. Buy the best you can afford; your life may depend upon it.

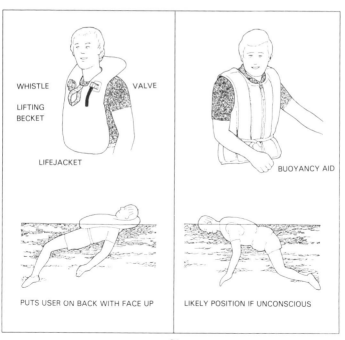

WHISTLE   VALVE

LIFTING
BECKET

LIFEJACKET

BUOYANCY AID

PUTS USER ON BACK WITH FACE UP

LIKELY POSITION IF UNCONSCIOUS

Buoyancy

A canoe stuffed full of buoyancy will not take in much water; water rolling around inside a canoe, as with any other craft, makes the boat very unstable. Many white-water canoeists prefer to fill every available space with air bags. Tailored air bags are obviously the best, but the foam blocks supporting the deck have to be removed. Bags are now being produced that fit around the blocks, avoiding the need to remove the blocks that are intended by the manufacturers to stiffen up the canoe. All buoyancy must be tied into the boat; an embarrassing situation occurs if the buoyancy floats out of the boat in the event of a capsize.

Chapter 3
Basic Techniques

Entry into a canoe presents a problem to the novice. The cockpit area is a bit restricted. The best launching place is a bed of sand or gravel with enough water to float the unloaded canoe, with deeper water just beyond. Sit on the rear deck and slide your legs into the cockpit, and then ease yourself into the boat. The lack of stability is an embarrassment, but one can brace oneself with a paddle across the deck or behind the rear of the cockpit.

Ease yourself into water of paddling depth, using your arms to 'walk' the boat into the water.

Entering the canoe. Photo: Brian Mitchinson

WALK CANOE INTO WATER

Paddling

Apart from being able to swim, good paddling technique is the most important canoeing skill.

For your initial paddling practice, try rolling the wrist to dip alternate blades. A push forward with the upper arm with the lower arm being used as a fulcrum develops more leverage in the stroke. This paddling method develops more power than the normal pull. Problems of stability and direction will have to be overcome and will get easier with practice. A paddle in the water acts as an out-rigger for your craft; canoeists call this a 'brace'. A small lean into the paddle when paddling on either side helps to keep direction and

PUSH

PADDLING
FULCRUM

Launching the canoe. Photo: Brian Mitchinson

saves using extra effort on one side or the other. With your toes on the foot-rest and knees under the deck, push on the down-side with the knees with alternate paddle strokes. This helps to maintain the balance of the boat.

Sweep Strokes

A change in direction is induced by a sweep stroke. Place the paddle in the water at the bow, sweep in a big arc, and exit the paddle at the stern. This will spin the canoe on its rockered bottom and so give a change of direction.

One forward sweep and a reverse sweep on the other side will spin the boat around without any forward motion.

Stopping the Canoe

To reduce the speed of the boat when travelling in a straight line, alternate dipping of the paddles followed by gentle reverse paddle strokes should be able to stop the canoe from speed in its own length.

Draw Strokes
To be able to move the boat sideways to effect a landing is a basic skill. Try it like this. Place the paddle in the water on the landing side, face parallel to the boat, and pull, so causing the boat to move sideways. If the boat over-runs the paddle, the canoeist will get wet! It is necessary to angle the blade and lift it out of the water before the boat over-runs the paddle. A lean into the paddle blade puts the boat on to its side and gives less water resistance.

Sculling Draw Strokes
A sculling draw if neatly executed looks impressive. No attempt is made to angle the boat. With the shaft vertical in the water the blade is angled and pulled, then returned with a rhythmic to-and-fro movement without exiting the water. A knee pressed up on the paddle side helps maintain the balance of the boat without tipping it, allowing the water to flow under the boat without hindrance.

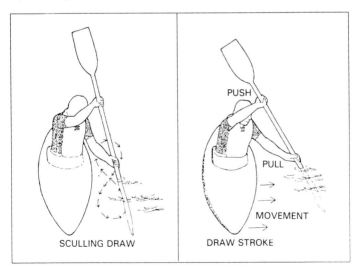

SCULLING DRAW | DRAW STROKE

Capsize Prevention
In fact, a capsize sooner or later is inevitable, but a canoeist will

always avoid one if possible. There are two basic ways of supporting your canoe and preventing it from turning over.

1. *Slap Support..* A recovery can be made by slapping the face of the paddle on the water as you approach an unstable position. This requires a quick reaction and is only obtained with practice.

2. *Sculling Support.* A more advanced recovery method is by sculling. The blade is angled in the water, so that it just skims the water surface. Forward and reverse sweeps are made until stability is regained. This is achieved on the down-side lean. With the feet on the foot-rest, push up with the knee on the cockpit coaming knee-brace, relaxing the other knee.

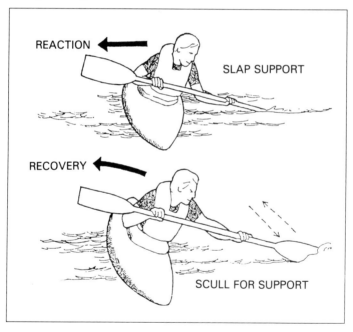

Stern Rudder

You have already learned how to do the sweep strokes. Paddle forward. Place the paddle as though you were going to do a reverse sweep, but instead of sweeping the paddle blade forward, hold it in

Stern Rudder. Photo: Brian Mitchinson

the water near the stern, and the canoe will turn towards that side.

Bow Rudder

For this stroke you place the blade as though you were going to do a forward sweep, but instead of sweeping the paddle towards the stern, hold it near the bow. This will turn the canoe towards the paddle. Be careful to have the face of the blade (that is, the driving side of the blade) facing towards the canoe. Then, when you have turned the canoe towards the way you want to go, you can immediately go on paddling.

Low Telemark

This is developed from the stern rudder. With the blade acting as a rudder, as the boat turns, sweep the blade forward and flatten it on the water amidships, leaning on the flattened blade.

On embarking in the canoe, facing upstream, it is usually necessary to break into the faster-flowing water in the centre of the river.

29

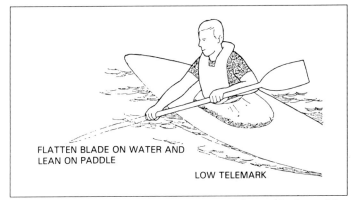

FLATTEN BLADE ON WATER AND
LEAN ON PADDLE

LOW TELEMARK

Paddle slowly forward until the current snatches at the bow of the boat, and then make a stern rudder which puts the bow into the faster stream. Sweep the paddle in a big arc, but while doing so flatten the blade, until the paddle lies amidships. Lean hard downstream. With the aid of the current the boat will be whipped round, to proceed downriver. This may seem rather desperate initially, so practise on still water. This stroke is very similar to a sweep stroke, except that you lean on a flattened blade. Push up with the knees to help recovery.

The great mistake a novice can make is to fail to lean downstream. If you are leaning upstream, water will hit the deck and 'water-wheel' you over, and a swim to the bank will result. To break out of fast water is another application of the same stroke.

Capsizing
Canoeists say that if you do not capsize you are not trying! The fear of the first capsize may inhibit your canoeing, so it is best to practise coping with the situation.

With the spray deck off, paddle into deep water. Put the paddle alongside the boat, place your hands on the deck behind the cockpit, roll over, and count to three. To make sure you are upside-down, push with your hands, lifting your seat out of the cockpit, rather like removing your trousers. Somersault out of the boat. Recover your paddle, grab the toggle-rope of the canoe and swim the boat ashore without righting it. Push the end of the boat well ashore, and lift the rear, and the boat will empty.

Re-embark, fit the spray deck, and repeat the capsize, holding on to the release tab. Place the hands on the deck at the rear of the cockpit, somersault out and proceed as before. Try this first in still water, then capsize in the river. Your confidence will increase with practice.

Attempting to get out of the boat before being completely upside-down will result in your bruising your legs on the cockpit area, and is the sign of a panic situation.

BRITISH CANOE UNION

The British Canoe Union is the governing body of canoe sport and has much to offer to even the casual canoeist.

The BCU controls all competitive canoeing, from canoe sailing and sprint racing to slalom and marathon racing. The novice may not be interested in the competitive side, but the advantage of joining lies in the strength of the Union to negotiate access to water, particularly as the fishing lobby has considerable strength when it comes to the use of rivers.

The BCU also offers good value in insurance cover for boats and equipment and third party insurance, which is advisable for a canoeist particularly when surfing from a beach.

The Union also conducts proficiency tests in both inland and sea canoeing, and qualifies instructors, senior instructors and coaches.

Proficiency Test

The proficiency test is a good standard for a novice to reach. The test is conducted on a river moving at approximately two miles per hour, and the candidate must present him/herself for the test with the boat and equipment in a serviceable condition. The candidate must satisfy the examiner:

1. that his canoe handing is proficient and that he can move the canoe sideways and prevent a capsize by the use of support strokes;
2. that he can ferry-glide his craft in fast water and break into and out of fast currents;
3. that he can capsize, recover equipment and empty the boat;
4. that he can swim 50 metres wearing a life-jacket in the prevailing water conditions;
5. that he can answer questions on good canoeing practice.

The holder of such a proficiency certificate would be a competent member of a canoeing party on a down-river trip.

There is also a progression for a keen canoeist to take an advanced test, with the possibility later of taking a course to become a senior instructor, qualifying through an examination, by maintaining a log book, and by demonstrating the ability to teach canoeing.

ACCESS TO WATER

The most difficult problem for a canoeist is to find a stretch of water where he is at least tolerated if not exactly made welcome.

Lakes

The beginner is well advised to launch himself into a quiet stretch of water from a shallow beach, and there gain confidence in the mastery of the canoe. A lake is probably the most suitable water for a novice. Some access for small boats on lakes and ponds has usually been negotiated by other boat owners. Look for a suitable launching point where the public has access to the lakeshore, and avoid trespassing on farm land. In the Lake District, for example, Ullswater and Windermere have a right of navigation, and the smaller lakes such as Coniston Water have stretches of shoreline owned by the National Trust, who welcome canoeists but not power-boat owners. But Wastwater and Buttermere are wholly owned by the National Trust who feel that on these lakes small boats are an intrusion on the landscape, and it is thought that they may restrict their use.

Be aware that in mountainous areas a placid lake can suddenly be turned into wild, rough water by a passing squall, leaving a chastened, shaken, or capsized canoeist as the water once again regains its calm. Keep a 'weather eye' open for the approach of a darkened patch of water which indicates the approach of a squall.

Canals

Canals in the U.K. are owned by the nationalised British Waterways Board, and a licence is needed to canoe them. The only white-water found on the 'Cut' is below the locks where foam from detergent is an indication of pollution. But rural stretches like those in the Welsh border region make pleasant paddling. The Brecon to Abergavenny Canal would make a nice contrast to a white-water trip on the River Usk.

Estuaries

Maps produced by the Ordnance Survey show the upper tidal limits of estuaries. This information is indispensable to the canoeist. There is normally a free right of passage. The map shows riverbanks in blue but delineates the tidal limits in black. Points of access are indicated by perhaps a ford or a road running alongside the bank, or under bridges where access is needed to repair the bridge.

As you leave the mature river, areas of mud are left at low tide. As the tide recedes swift current and over-falls present difficulties and perhaps danger to the unwary canoeist.

There are also problems of exit from an estuary. It is always better to reconnoitre the way out, possibly by means of a side steam, before the journey is undertaken.

Rivers

In the Lake District some rivers were used for transporting slate and minerals and so have navigation rights. The lower Leven and the Brathay were used for transporting gunpowder, a very unstable material and particularly unsafe on roads. The River Crake, the outlet from Coniston Water, was used for transporting slate, which was loaded in Coniston village and ferried down the lake and into the river to be transhipped into barges at Greenodd, where the gunpowder also was loaded. The River Duddon is assumed to have been used for transporting charcoal produced in the woodland along the river banks to the huge charcoal-fired furnace at Duddon Bridge.

Access to the rivers must be over public land, as must egress. Trespassing on private land gives the sport a bad name. In Scotland the law of trespass is rather different. It is often possible to find a stretch of water locally, where wild-water canoeing can be practised without causing annoyance to either landowners or fishermen.

Chapter 4
Hazards

A river, even one that is well known, will change its character completely after heavy rain. It is as well always to be prepared for such a changed situation. Having worked out a problem beforehand, the canoeist is in a better position to cope with a similar problem in an emergency and remain cool. You must practise the techniques necessary to handle hazards and not wait for the problems to arise.

Capsize
In the event of a capsize you must KEEP CALM.

Stay with the boat; do not attempt to right it. Swim to the rear end, against the current, and angle the boat to the river. The current will then push the canoe to the bank, as in the 'ferry glide' (see Chapter 5). If you are in danger of being swept over a weir, it is probably better to let the boat go, swim upstream in the 'ferry glide' position and so gain the river bank.

A capsize in open water is not a difficult proposition if you are a member of a party. Go for the Eskimo rescue position. Stay in the

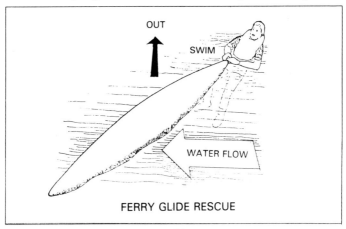

OUT

SWIM

WATER FLOW

FERRY GLIDE RESCUE

boat upside-down, hands out of the water. With luck, a paddler will present a bow to either hand, which will help you to roll yourself up. Pause to take a breath for the strength to haul yourself upright. If you exit your canoe you will require the assistance of a number of canoeists to regain a seat in your boat, with the risk of exposure.

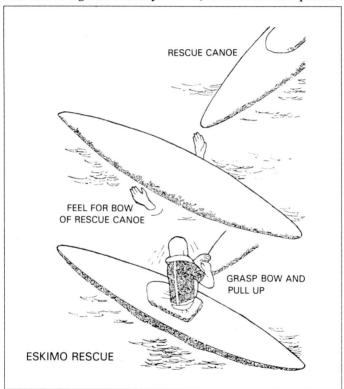

RESCUE CANOE

FEEL FOR BOW OF RESCUE CANOE

GRASP BOW AND PULL UP

ESKIMO RESCUE

Stuck between Boulders

In a boulder-strewn river, it is only too easy to be caught broadside on to the river and be trapped between two boulders. Self-rescue is virtually impossible, but lean vigorously downstream and wait until rescuers can lift the bow or stern off. If the boat is abandoned with a lean upstream, the water will enter the cockpit and the pressure will burst the boat open.

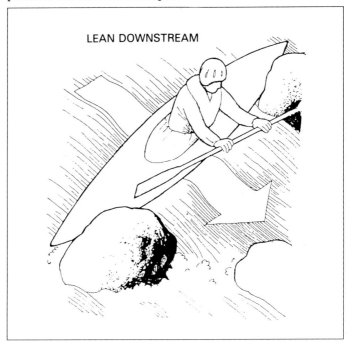

LEAN DOWNSTREAM

Swept under Trees

A fast-flowing river tends to undercut its banks, and a tree which would not normally be in the water could well be submerged in spate conditions with water sucking down through the branches. If the paddler finds himself in this situation with his canoe swept into the branches, the only answer is to abandon the boat and climb into the branches. Such a situation is best avoided; but it has happened.

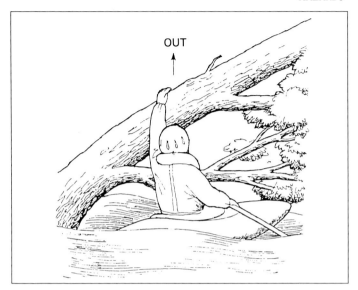

Stuck in a Stopper

If the canoeist finds himself stuck broadside on in a stopper, he is in a difficult situation. A high brace over the top of the stopper wave may gain a release, but with a wave of any size there is little hope of pulling out over the top. Try to work the boat to the end of the stopper, where there could be a release or rescue.

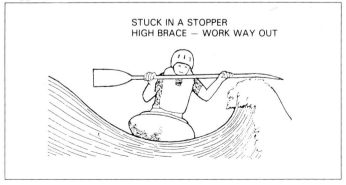

Tip-out

An even more unpleasant situation is to be unexpectedly tipped out

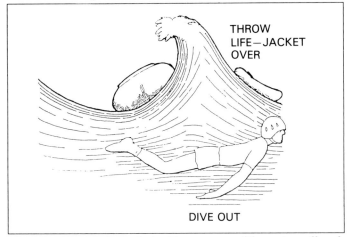

THROW
LIFE—JACKET
OVER

DIVE OUT

of your boat in or below a chute. The pressure of the water will suck you down, and then up on the face of the stopper wave, to be recirculated back into the hole. Try to work your way to the bank. Friends should try tying a line to a life-jacket and throwing it into the stopper, to pull you in. If help is not available, then as a last resort remove your life-jacket, throw it over the stopper wave, and dive deep and out, recovering the life-jacket on the other side.

Weirs

Canoeists have drowned in and around weirs. The power of the water going over even a small weir makes rescue difficult. Danger lies in capsizing in fast water and failing to roll first time, resulting in being dragged uncontrollably through boulder chokes. A crash helmet is a necessity, and help on the river bank is also important, if only to recover the canoe or paddle abandoned by the canoeist. It is obviously foolish to canoe alone. On top slalom courses, a wet-suited diver is positioned at the bottom of every hazard. Underwater obstructions are common below weirs in big rivers; find out about them before launching. Always take the right line - a failure to follow it may result in the canoeist sitting on the sill of the weir

Over the sill in a polyethylene boat. Photo: Brian Mitchinson

with the water rushing round him, the only escape being to fall into the hole below the weir with an inevitable capsize. In this case stay in the canoe for a few seconds and hope to be dragged clear of the stopper wave before attempting to roll.

Canoeing in a group is essential on rapid rivers. A difficult section should first be inspected from the bank, the leader making the first

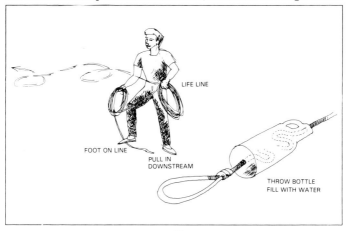

39

run before the others embark. The leader then directs from the pool below, a life-line ready. The group attempts the run one at a time, waiting for any difficulty to clear, with the most experienced canoeist bringing up the rear. Portage is advised for novice canoeists.

Exposure

Exposure is a hazard which should not be regarded lightly, for even on a warm summer's day there is a risk of exposure. Hypothermia, as it is often called, is well understood by mountaineers but tends to be disregarded by water-sport enthusiasts. The condition is best avoided rather than treated.

The human system needs food and drink to produce energy and body heat, and a failure to be adequately fed significantly increases the risk of exposure. What is more important is the need to be suitably clothed. A breeze blowing over an exposed body reduces the body temperature, and more so if the body surface is wet. This can be demonstrated by blowing air from a vacuum cleaner over a thermometer and noticing the temperature drop. Wetting the thermometer bulb will give an even greater temperature drop. It is very important that the canoeist wears a windproof garment on the upper body, even when wearing a wet-suit.

If it is suspected that a companion is beginning to suffer from exposure, either through repeated capsizing or irrational behaviour or even a failure to keep up with the rest of the party, action must be taken immediately. Serious symptoms are uncontrollable shivering, slurred speech, and double vision. Make for shore and rest. Provide hot drinks and food and additional clothing; it is not necessary to remove the wet clothes, as water is a good insulator. Persuade the victim to get into an exposure bag to warm up, and suspend the trip even though the person claims to have a feeling of well-being.

The outer layers of the body have chilled and have started to take away heat from the inner core, and this condition is dangerous. In a serious case death may result. Call a doctor and arrange immediate evacuation of the victim. Hospital treatment is the only remedy.

Chapter 5
Reading the Water

The canoeist uses the power of the river to propel his boat, and a wise canoeist will use the flow to turn his canoe, assisted by the paddle. A knowledge of the interaction of water with river banks and bed is part of the canoeist's basic skill.

The canal has 'flow', due to the occasional opening of the lock gates at its lower level, and being of uniform depth and width the flow is uniform over its whole section.

A river has varying depths, as well as obstructions on the bed, and normally takes a winding course. The 'flow rate' will differ with the depth. Rivers speed up on the outside of bends, and obstructions in the river cause the water flow to be diverted.

On a down-stream passage the canoeist will need to identify the

White water canoeing in a bat boat.
Photo: Brian Mitchinson

main stream. On a quiet stretch of water the river will normally be deep, but on approaching turbulent water, a 'V' in the water flow will lead to the deeper section. Any 'standing waves' indicate a submerged boulder. Approaching a bend, the deepest channel is to be found on the outside of the curve, with shallows and shingle on the inside of the bend. As rivers increase in speed, the paddler will see boulders on the river bed, with a cushion of water piling up in front of them which will push a floating object to one side. Downstream of the boulder there will be a 'return flow' of water, filling the hole made by the obstructing boulder. The canoeist can use this return flow. Pull in behind the rock, and in this eddy current the bow

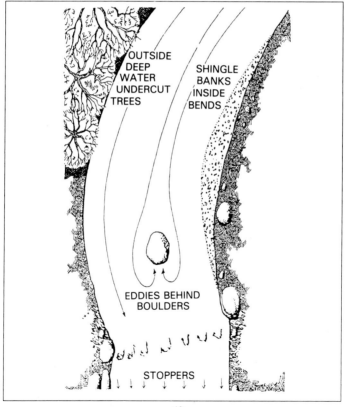

OUTSIDE DEEP WATER UNDERCUT TREES

SHINGLE BANKS INSIDE BENDS

EDDIES BEHIND BOULDERS

STOPPERS

Running the Brathay. Photo: Brian Mitchinson

will be pulled in close to the boulder, where the canoeist can take a rest.

As the river gains in volume, water sweeps over a 'sill' in a smooth stream of considerable force, its passage being confined by boulder 'chokes' on either side. At the bottom of the 'spout' or 'V', white standing waves will form as the water deepens, usually as a big wave followed by two or three smaller ones. In these cases the canoeist is well advised to land and inspect before making a passage. It will be observed that the first of the waves below the spout will curl over upstream (a vertical eddy known as a 'stopper'). The secondary stoppers are also curling over but without the power of the first. There will be a return of water on either side of the spout ('eddy currents'), adding to the power of the stopper wave. When

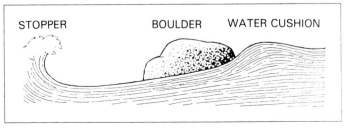

shooting a spout, paddle hard. On hitting the stopper wave speed will be considerably reduced, and without the initial spurt to help him the canoeist can be thrown back into the hole that precedes the stopper. Below spouts canoeists like to play and improve their techniques, but shooting a spout needs considerable experience and some caution.

As the river matures, weirs are often constructed which frequently can be shot after an inspection. When shooting a weir, brace against the foot-rest and lean well back. The 'boil' of water below a weir is well aerated with water moving upwards with large volumes of air bubbles, and a feeling of instability and lack of power results. Have a care, for weirs are dangerous places, producing stoppers which can drown you.

Breaking In and Breaking Out

Below a suitable spout, paddle upstream into the return eddies, and with a stern rudder angle the bow into the spout of the water; as the boat swings round sweep your paddle amidships, lean downhill on a flat blade and break into the current. To break out, use a stern rudder; as the bow hits the return eddy, sweep the paddle amidships on a flattened blade and lean uphill against the stream of water. This move calls for nicely judged timing, as the wrong lean, say into the stream of water, will make a capsize inevitable.

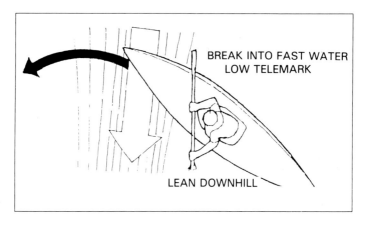

BREAK INTO FAST WATER
LOW TELEMARK

LEAN DOWNHILL

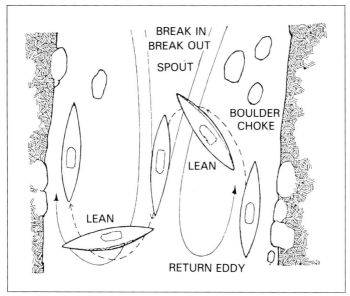

Ferry Glides

A 'ferry glide' gets its name from an old-established method of operating a ferry in a fast-flowing stream. A chain or line across the river was secured on both banks, with a pulley running on it to which a boat was tied. The ferry-boat was ruddered into the main stream and the water flow impinging on the side of the boat pushed it across - a ferry from bank to bank with no fuel and no effort. The principle you use is the same.

Upstream Ferry Glide. Paddle the boat out into the main stream. Angle the boat relative to the water flow, paddle slowly forward, and the water will push the canoe across. Reverse the direction of the angle and the boat will cross back. No effort, no bother.

Reverse Ferry Glide. This is rather more difficult. Draw the stern out at an angle to the main stream, back paddle gently to maintain your position relative to the bank, and the boat will be pushed across. This is a convenient way of inspecting a 'line' down a river before committing yourself to the descent. Practise this on varying speeds of river, until you get the hang of it.

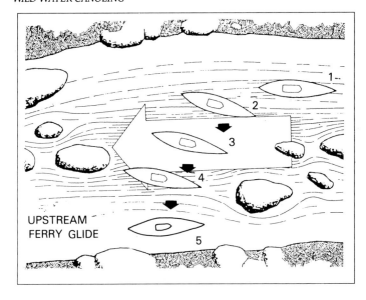

Use of Eddies and Stopper Waves

To make progress upstream would be almost impossible in the main current, but by observing where the return flow of water occurs, progress upstream can be made with very little effort. Selecting a back eddy behind a boulder, you paddle up it until the water hole is reached; here the canoe will be held in behind the boulder and you can take a rest. In the main stream over a sill a secondary stopper wave is formed. Perch on this wave amidships, and the returning vertical eddy will hold the canoe in position amid a seething mass of water. With a neat angled draw or cross-bow rudder the paddler will be propelled across the river into a returning 'back eddy' of the inside bend in the river; thus progress is made upstream. This, as you will gather, is a skill not learnt overnight, but practise it on slower streams and you will find the technique relatively easy.

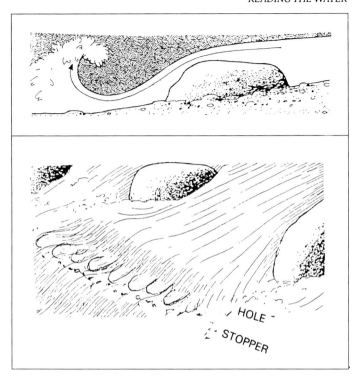

HOLE -

STOPPER

Slalom

On a river where natural hazards occur, organised canoeists like to play. Sets of two poles hanging vertically are strung from bank to bank, with a gap of three or four feet between the poles. Through these gates a canoe in competition must pass without touching the poles. In top-ranking slalom courses the poles are placed in the most difficult eddies just clear of the water. The gates must be taken in either a forward or a reverse direction in a prescribed order. Touching a pole will incur a time penalty, and the winner is the canoeist who completes the fastest run of two with the time penalty added for touching the gates.

Slalom boats are usually of extreme design with a low profile and

47

pronounced rocker, described by canoeists as a wet boat. They are usually made from fibre-glass reinforced with other fibres and are produced individually on small production lines. Competitive canoeing requires ever-changing designs.

Using low-volume boats, competitors progress from novice events to first division competitions using the technique of dipping stern and bow to avoid touching the gates. The division system ensures that competitors are of the same standard.

Down-river Racing

For this type of canoeing, boats are specifically designed with straight keels and arrow-shaped plan, and are constructed to meet the prescribed width specification. The canoeist selects a line down the river following the main stream and avoiding all eddies. The winner is the canoeist who survives the course in the fastest time.

Playing in a stopper at Holme Pierepoint.
Photo: Frank Goodman, Valley Canoe Products. Canoeist: Mike Devlin

Chapter 6
Advanced Techniques

In heavy water, high paddle strokes dig deeper into the faster-flowing stream of water which lies under the aerated white foam - which has no substance - found in rapid rivers.

Hanging Turns
Here the blade is placed in the water a little way in front of you, barely before the end of the cockpit. The whole paddle is more or less vertical if looked at from the bow, but slopes slightly backwards towards your shoulder if looked at from the side. The blade in the water must be opened slightly and feel for the pressure of the water on the blade, thus acting as a rudder. Be careful not to open it too far, as this will stop the canoe from turning. This is the best stroke for turning the canoe. It is constantly used in deep water, but it is not a satisfactory stroke in surf, when a stern rudder comes into its own.

High Draw
With a vertical shaft the arms outstretched, plunge the paddle into

HIGH DRAW TO PULL OUT OF A SMALL STOPPER

the water amidships, with the face of the blade parallel to the canoe. With a vigorous lean into the paddle, pull with the bottom hand and push with the top. The boat is propelled towards the paddle, and with a smart flick of the hips and a push with the knee on the downhill side of the cockpit coaming, one recovers stability.

This basic stroke is modified in a number of ways by angling the submerged blade. The paddle then acts as a rudder and induces a turn known as a 'draw turn'. By moving the paddle action towards the stern and putting your weight back, you lift the bow of the canoe a little and execute a very quick turn known as a 'hanging turn'.

High Telemark

The high telemark turn is another hanging stroke based on the vertical shaft. It is particularly useful when the canoeist wants to

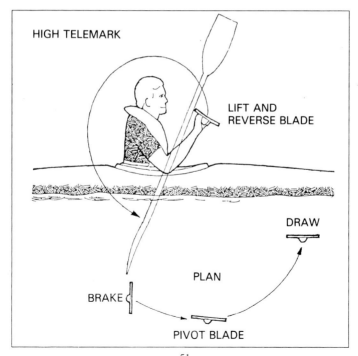

HIGH TELEMARK

LIFT AND
REVERSE BLADE

DRAW

PLAN

BRAKE

PIVOT BLADE

cut out of the main stream of the river into an eddy, the returning water behind a boulder.

The action is to raise both arms grasping the paddle above the head and thus rotate the paddle blades into a reverse position. Drop the blade into the water to the rear of the cockpit, with the blade at right angles to the canoe, and lean back. This acts as a brake. Keeping the shaft vertical and leaning towards the paddle, move it round in an arc, pivoting the blade as you do so, and finish with a powerful draw at the forward end of the cockpit. Some canoeists move the upper arm behind the head, but this is not really necessary and puts the paddle in a difficult position in the event of a capsize while doing the stroke.

High Support Stroke

If the paddler gets out of balance when attempting high strokes, a high support stroke can gain a recovery. Basically it is rather similar to the 'high draw'. A strong pull on the vertical shaft will produce sufficient reaction, and with a smart hip flick and a push with the knee under the cockpit coaming initiated by the foot on the foot-rest, recovery is quite easy. It is quite possible to perform a roll on this stroke, known as the 'storm roll'.

Cross-bow Rudders

With a cross-bow rudder, apart from the feeling of instability, the pull is not as great if the paddle is raised to a vertical shaft with the blade angled to change direction, but it makes a useful stroke to practise with.

Combining Strokes

A skilled canoeist, with a combination of high strokes, can weave his way through the water without lifting the paddle out. For example, he can change the high telemark into a bow rudder to gain the exact position required in an eddy, ready for the next move in a boulder-choked stream or a slalom course. At this stage of the sport the boat becomes an extension of the body of the paddler. This is achieved by gripping the boat with the thighs and rolling the hips from side to side, with alternate pumping of the knees against the knee-braces in the canoe. Working the feet on the foot-rest, the whole body con-tributes towards the power stroke of the paddler. The canoeist

BOW RUDDER

CROSS BOW RUDDER

positions himself in the water with only body leans and support from the paddle.

High Cross

The high cross is used to cross from one eddy to another over a stopper wave. If you want to try surfing, this is the technique to use.

Having mastered high strokes, and not before, the canoeist can move into more rapid water. Select a suitable spout and aim for the first wave; draw into it and attempt to surf, which requires a delicate balance. Perched on the wave amidships, aim to maintain your position by angling the blade of the paddle as in the hanging stroke. One can then move the boat across the face of the wave in either direction, from one bank to the other. But have a care! On a big wave, if you drive too far forward, the bow of the canoe will dive into the surging chute of water, the stern will lift, and a loop will result. This is rather interesting if done deliberately but not at all amusing if unintended.

Chapter 7
Rolls and Rescues

The ability to conduct a self-rescue is the greatest safety factor in canoe sport. It is usually the lack of confidence rather than the lack of ability to perform the feat which hinders self-rescue. Confidence-building is an important part of self-rescue.

With a friend standing alongside the boat in waist-deep water, place your head on the fore-deck and arms round the hull of the boat, and capsize. The friend immediately rolls the boat up, which is easy to do as the centre of gravity is low providing the canoeist holds on to the bottom of the boat.

Continue to practise as follows. Capsize, count three, tap on the bottom of the boat and hang on; your friend then rolls the boat up. As confidence in the friend improves, capsize and count twenty — thirty — forty seconds before you hammer on the bottom of the boat and your friend rolls you up. A face mask or nose clip helps.

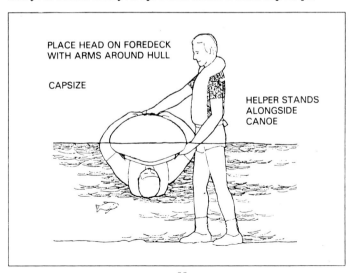

PLACE HEAD ON FOREDECK
WITH ARMS AROUND HULL

CAPSIZE

HELPER STANDS
ALONGSIDE
CANOE

Self-Rescue

With the spray-deck on, capsize. Without leaving the boat, swim using arm strokes (dog paddle or breast stroke), and swim for the bank. At the bank, keep your weight low, leaning either forward or back on to the deck, and push yourself into an upright position from the bed of the river.

SELF RESCUE

Eskimo Rescue

A convenient way to avoid getting out of the boat after a failed roll is to use the Eskimo rescue method as described already. By hammering with the hands on the bottom of your upturned boat, the attention of other canoeists is drawn, to present a bow and so gain a recovery.Then you can continue the practice without the hassle of re-embarking in the canoe and fitting a spray-deck.

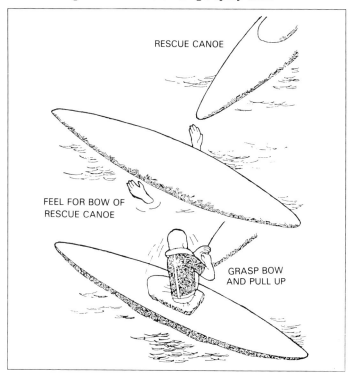

RESCUE CANOE

FEEL FOR BOW OF
RESCUE CANOE

GRASP BOW
AND PULL UP

Eskimo Rolls: The Pawlata Method

There are several methods of performing the Eskimo roll. The easiest to learn is a roll developed by an Austrian canoeist named Pawlata. Some people can pick up the roll quite easily, while other

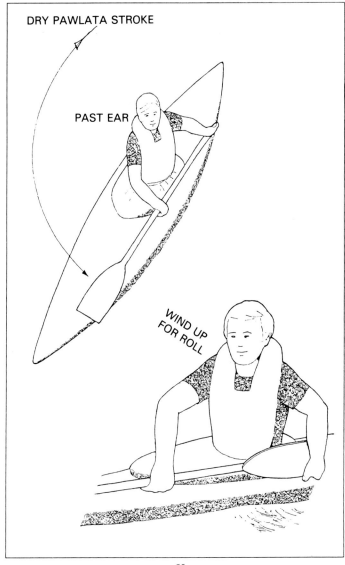

DRY PAWLATA STROKE

PAST EAR

WIND UP FOR ROLL

folk have considerable difficulty, but basically it needs to be learnt with the assistance of a partner standing alongside the boat to roll the canoe up if the roll fails. Remember that hanging on to the bottom of the canoe makes rescue easy. Having experimented with self-rescue your confidence under water should be much improved before you try to roll.

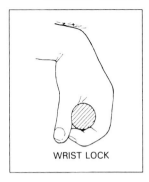

WRIST LOCK

Start by mastering the stroke itself. With the paddle blade resting on the deck by the bow, grasp the paddle shaft and twist the wrist. Grasp the other paddle blade rather like holding a guitar, with the arm twisted over the front of the blade. Lean forward, keeping your arms straight, and lift the forward arm until the biceps touch the ear. Look at the sketch and practise the movement dry. Then, in shallow water or a swimming pool, with an assistant standing by in water about waist deep, practise the roll as follows.

With the paddle blade on the deck, hollow face up, lean forward. The assistant, standing by the bow, grasps the paddle blade, and you capsize. The assistant passes the blade under the boat as the canoeist capsizes. Observe the position of the blade on the water. STRIKE, biceps passing ear. The assistant hangs on to the blade,

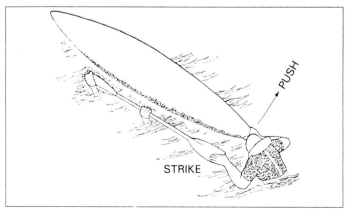

PUSH

STRIKE

pushing the bow away; and as you surface, lean back with your head on the rear deck, to help stability. Practise a few times, observing the position of the blade as it starts its stroke. Watch the paddle slice through the water as the arms unwind, and with a supple hip movement, head back on the rear deck, you will surface; and to regain stability twist the wrist and arc the blade forward as in a support stoke.

Hip Flick
It helps to complete the roll with the movement known as a hip flick. This needs to be practised. With an assistant standing alongside the boat, tip the boat with the weight on the paddle. Now try to place the boat flat on the water and follow through with the body, leaning backwards or forwards to keep a low centre of gravity. The movement is a flick of the hips. Some people do this quite naturally and succeed after a few attempts.

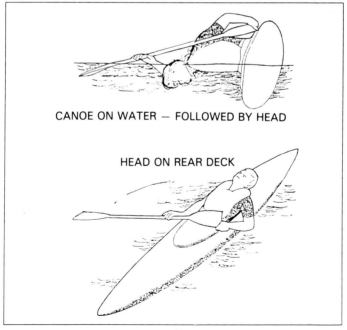

CANOE ON WATER — FOLLOWED BY HEAD

HEAD ON REAR DECK

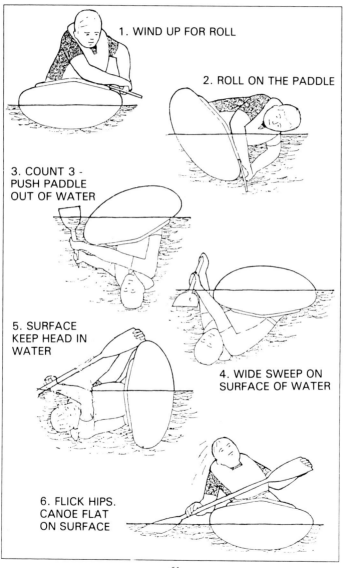

1. WIND UP FOR ROLL

2. ROLL ON THE PADDLE

3. COUNT 3 - PUSH PADDLE OUT OF WATER

5. SURFACE KEEP HEAD IN WATER

4. WIDE SWEEP ON SURFACE OF WATER

6. FLICK HIPS. CANOE FLAT ON SURFACE

Some Tips

Aim to watch the blade striking through the water. On completing the stroke look at the bed of the river; this ensures that your head is kept down as the boat is placed upright on the surface of the water. Follow through with your body, leaning back on the deck of the canoe.

Causes of Failure

1. Paddle blade initially on wrong side of boat.
2. Paddle sinks to bottom of river. Angle wrong. The blade must skim the surface throughout the stroke.
3. You surface but cannot recover. Centre of gravity too high. You must lean back, head on the rear deck.
   Persist, and the roll will be successful.

Screw Roll

Having succeeded with the Pawlata roll which uses a long lever, try a roll gripping the paddle in the normal position. The stoke is exactly the same, but uses a short lever. In the capsize position, push the whole paddle out of the water and then strike. The roll will be complete.

If you fail to push the whole paddle out of the water, the inactive blade will get trapped under the canoe and the roll will fail. Practise rolling both left and right-hand.

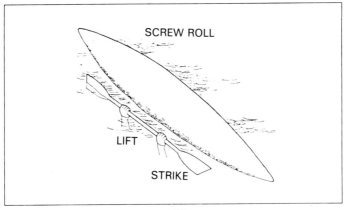

Other rolls are: 'storm roll', which operates with a vertical shaft and is used in very rough water.

'Steyr roll', which starts from a laid-back position.

'Pull-across roll', which is thought to have been the original Eskimo roll.

Deep-water Rescues

Sometimes a canoeist will capsize and be unable to roll his canoe up again and will have to get out. If he is far from land, in a large lake for instance, his canoe will have to be emptied of water and himself put back into the boat. There are a number of ways of achieving this, known as deep-water rescues, but most of them are only suitable for experienced paddlers. Each method has its own benefits and pitfalls, and therefore each one is more or less appropriate in particular circumstances. The 'raft-tee' method shown in the diagram is a common fail-safe method which can be confidently recommended for general use.

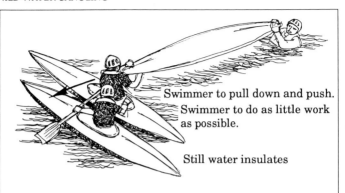

Swimmer to pull down and push.
Swimmer to do as little work
as possible.

Still water insulates

TWO CANOE RAFT
Second man supporting rescuer
with paddles across decks
and holding onto cockpit coaming.

Rock boat to empty the water
completely out, then turn the
right way up.

Assist swimmer into his boat.
Replace the spray-deck.
Stability is maintained by
paddles across the decks.

Chapter 8
River Touring

River touring takes some organising and forethought: seek out information about your chosen river. It is necessary first to find out about the access situation and approach to the British Canoe Union will give an indication of the problems that you are likely to encounter with landlords and riparian owners.

Ensure that your party is competent for the trip and equal to the difficulties of your river. Rivers are graded as to difficulty from one to six.

Grade one rivers are described as easy, with occasional small rapids, waves regular and low; correct course easy to find, but care needed with obstacles such as pebble banks, protective works, fallen trees, etc., especially on narrow rivers.

Grade two. Medium; fairly frequent rapids, usually with regular waves, easy eddies or whirlpools; course generally easy to recognise.

Grade three. Difficult; rapids numerous with fairly high irregular waves, broken water, eddies and whirlpools; course not easily recognisable.

Grade four. Very difficult; long and extended rapids with high irregular waves, difficult broken water, eddies and whirlpools; course often difficult to recognise; inspection from the bank always necessary.

Grade five. Exceedingly difficult; long unbroken stretches of rapids with difficult and completely irregular waves, submerged rocks and very fast eddies; previous inspection absolutely essential.

Grade six. The absolute limit of difficulty; all previously mentioned difficulties increased to the limit of practicability; cannot be attempted without risk to life.

Your chosen river may well contain stretches of all these grades, so it is really essential to research it thoroughly.

If Youth Hostels are available along the bank of the river it solves the problem of transporting heavy gear. If not, camping will have to be considered. Will the party carry their tents with them, or will

The joy of heavy water canoeing. Photo: Gaybo Ltd.

they have a support party of non-canoeists to find their campsites and organise the food? A good deal of thought will have to be given as to the length of the day's journey and arrangements made for cooking and meeting the transport at the end of the day's paddle.

Packing a Canoe

To have completed a journey and then pull out a mess of soggy gear is an experience to be avoided. Forethought is essential. All gear carried in a canoe must be packed in waterproof containers. A satisfactory way is to use bin liners or (clean!) fertiliser bags. Pack

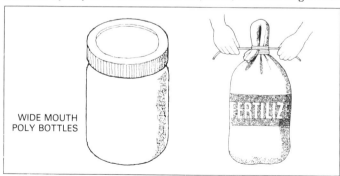

WIDE MOUTH
POLY BOTTLES

FERTILIZ

your gear in the plastic bag, bunch the top and inflate it. Tie the top, fold it over and tie again. If the bag deflates, discard it; and to be doubly safe pack the bag into a second bag and tie as before. These bags must be tied into the canoe in the order in which they are needed, so that last in (food and cooking utensils) means first out to be used on the journey.

Bags must not obstruct the feet or body in any way as to impede rapid exit from the canoe. Small gear can be packed in wide-mouthed polythene containers, but be sure to check that the seal on the lid is good.

Repairs to Canoes

Some damage will be experienced on any journey, and repairs will be needed on the spot. With fibre-glass or polyethylene boats, a satisfactory repair can be made with two-inch wide PVC sticky tape, but on longer journeys it would be wise to carry a fibre-glass repair kit, containing a small tin of resin and some hardener and glass-fibre mat. A useful way of drying the boat for repair is to pour methylated spirits over the area and allow it to evaporate.

A quick method of repairing a damaged area with the fibre-glass repair kit uses a polythene bag. Place the glass mat in the bag, pour in the resin and add the hardener; wet the mat with the resin inside the bag by squeezing with your fingers. Cut open the bag and use the polythene as backing to lay the resin-wetted mat on to the boat, working out the air from the edges of the bag with the hands. Leave the bag in place, and allow the resin to dry, before putting the boat back in the water.

First Aid

A first aid kit should always be carried, probably containing plasters, a triangular bandage, some safety pins, scissors, needle and cotton, and a burn dressing. All these items should be packed in a waterproof polythene bottle labelled "First Aid".

Transporting Canoes

Canoes can be carried on the roof rack of a car, placed the right way up with a spray-deck fitted. Rope them across the front and rear of the cockpit and tie to the roof rack. With this lashing the boats tend to 'float' at speed on the rushing air projected from the car's

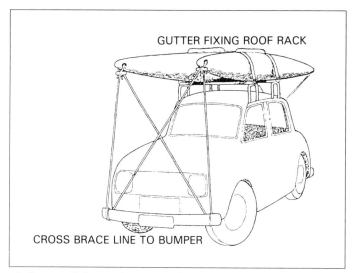

GUTTER FIXING ROOF RACK

CROSS BRACE LINE TO BUMPER

windscreen. It is very important that the front of the boat is tied to the car's bumper to prevent the boats swinging sideways. Use a cross-bracing method, knotted off at the canoes' toggles. The rear of the boats also can be tied down as an added precaution.

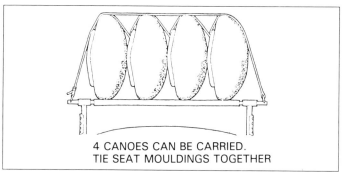

4 CANOES CAN BE CARRIED.
TIE SEAT MOULDINGS TOGETHER

Three or four canoes can be carried without difficutly placed on their sides; tie off the seat of one to the seat of the next, before lashing down to the roof rack and bumper. Paddles also can be carried in the cockpits, but the exposed blades must be at the rear of the car. Take care, and be warned that luggage elastics are unreliable and dangerous, and that some ropes stretch in the wet. Check your lashings regularly. There are many canoe casualties on motorways.

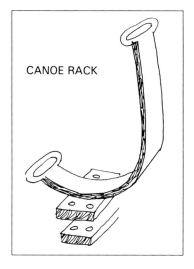

CANOE RACK

Where to go

Touring rivers in England are sparse, and all have problems with sport fishermen in the upper reaches. The classic trips which are used by commercial canoeing companies are on the Wye or the Severn.

In Scotland the position is much clearer after the Freshwater v Wills court case, where an injuction was sought to prevent canoeing on a stretch of the River Spey. After many months of hearings, the right was established for the passage of canoes. It was then taken to the House of Lords and upheld that there is a right of passage for canoes to pass and re-pass, though not to practise in one stretch of water. Canoeists in Scotland now claim the right of access on all rivers, and ask that permission is not sought to run a stretch, although they suggest that every courtesy is shown to fishermen who use the rivers. An injuction could be obtained preventing you as an individual from canoeing a stretch of water.

In the Lake District some rivers were used for transporting slate and minerals and so have right of navigation. The upper Derwent runs through National Trust property, and the N.T. has no objection to canoeists; and of course the lakes are there, provided that you have right of access to the shore without trespassing across private land. When there are no objections to canoeists, and often with local access agreements touring trips can be arranged. Membership of the British Canoe Union entitles you to local and national information supplied by its local river advisers. Where an old navigation

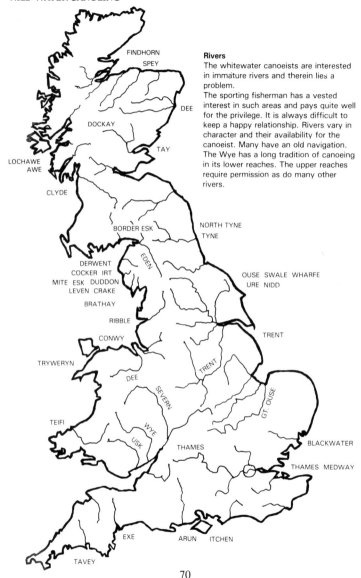

Rivers
The whitewater canoeists are interested in immature rivers and therein lies a problem.
The sporting fisherman has a vested interest in such areas and pays quite well for the privilege. It is always difficult to keep a happy relationship. Rivers vary in character and their availability for the canoeist. The Wye has a long tradition of canoeing in its lower reaches. The upper reaches require permission as do many other rivers.

exists on a river, there is a right to canoe. Examples are the Worcestershire Avon, the Severn, and the Ouse; in the southern counties, a stretch of the Itchen, and the Dart in Devon, where canoe sport can be had below the weirs.

Touring Abroad

Most mature rivers in Europe are used for navigation, but battling with commercial craft has its problems. The white-water canoeist is more interested in the rivers of the mountain regions, where water conditions can change during the day. An early morning flow can be quite moderate, but as the heat of the day causes the snow to melt in the higher mountains, the river can rise to full spate with the addition of localised thunderstorms. A further hazard is the local hydro-electric scheme that can turn a well-known river run into a highly hazardous undertaking by the following year. Continental river guides appear to become quickly out of date, and a number of British canoeists have drowned through either misunderstanding information given or ignoring it. On well-known slalom courses, canoeists have put in above well-recorded hazards rather than below.

It is very important to inspect personally all difficult sections, ignoring the advise of friends, whose "Oh, it will canoe alright", in my experience has put a party at serious risk. A bank support party with throw lines is an advisable precaution.

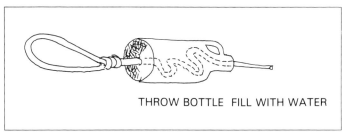

THROW BOTTLE FILL WITH WATER

A journey of a few kilometres is an expected day's travel. Heavy gear should be transported by vehicle rather than risk carrying heavy loads in the canoes in difficult water. Language difficulties could risk canoes being impounded by the local police for apparently no reason at all other than that you have infringed local fishing laws. Exit from the river is often quite difficult in warmer climes because of algal growth on the rocks making them very slippery. A well-briefed back-up team trained in rescue techniques is an essential requirement of the party. Remember you will encounter boulder chokes, rivers that disappear underground, narrow gorges, powerful over-falls, weirs, and very, very cold water.

In England the law relating to access is unproven, but some points are made and are published in the magazine of the British Canoe Union. As mentioned earlier, in Scotland it is proven by the appeal to the House of Lords and will probably go unchallenged. On the continent - who knows?

Ecology
The passage of canoeists should do little to disturb the wildlife close by or cause damage to the banks. A cautious, quiet approach may be rewarded by a glimpse of an otter sliding down the riverbank, or of a water vole with its glossy fur searching for food. A dipper may be witnessed curtseying on a rock before walking underwater (observe the shuttered eye) in search of freshwater animals, or the vivid blue-green flash as the kingfisher darts from branch to branch.

Regrettably some canoeing groups miss these sights. They accompany their passage along the waterway with shouts and yells as a release of tension, disturbing not only the wildlife but also other water users in search of tranquility.

"Have You a Right?"
(The following article by the author is reprinted from "Canoe Focus", the magazine of the British Canoe Union.)

When I arrived in the Lakes with a 17ft. folding canoe, the first thing I wanted to know was, "Have I a right?" A little local history research informed me that there was an old town wharf on the banks of the River Duddon.

Assuming that there was wharfage, there must have been shipping on the river, although the shingle banks suggest that it was a difficult navigation, but rivers may change and the right to navigate still exists - once a right, always a right. Further local research revealed that this was a busy navigation, with sailing barges often bow-hauled over shallow stretches, with brushwood behind the boat holding the water, thus acting as a lock stopping the river flow to make passage easier.

Considerable volumes of iron ore and limestone were transported up to Duddon Bridge to feed the huge hearth of Duddon Furnace, and, no doubt, iron pigs were shipped out the same way. An irrefutable argument to anglers who own the fishing rights on this stretch of the river. The Duddon Furnace was in fact fuelled by charcoal, of which a vast tonnage was needed to produce a ton of iron; the coppiced woodland can still be seen higher up the Duddon Valley and the pitsteads can be found alongside the river bank where the wood was carbonised to produce charcoal. This is a high-volume low-weight material, and transporting it using the muddy narrow roads and tracks used by packhorses in the 17th and 18th centuries would have been an impossible problem, but the river is there!

The obvious answer is that it was rafted down the Duddon to the furnace; many such small navigations exist in the Lakes. The River Crake was used for transporting slate down to Greenodd where it was transhipped into barges. Evidence of this transport system is shown by slates in the river bed, and the barge wharfage can still be seen with iron rings let into the bed-rock on the foreshore of the estuary.

Running the Brathay. Photo: Brian Mitchinson

Gunpowder was transported down the Brathay from Elterwater, exiting into Windermere from where it was forwarded to other parts of the country, by safer roads than the country roads or by rail.

A canoeist looking at his locality can often discover evidence of old navigations. First, one should realise that transport by road before tarmacadam was very difficult, the roads being very rutted and often "mud up". Wheeled vehicles pulled by huge teams of horses would have had great difficulty making any progress at all.

Look at your riverbanks; often a riverside path could indicate a tow-path for horse-hauled or human bow-hauled rafting, transporting heavy materials from site to site. The river route is often meandering and would not have been used for short cuts for ploughmen finding their way home after a hard day in the fields. Riverside walking is only a recent occurrence; a countryman would not have had the time or energy for a riverside walk, although he might take a trip in the dark in pursuit of fish.

These riverside paths are now used by anglers and walkers for recreation but one must realise they were in existence generations ago when recreation was a physical impossibility after working six days a week, twelve hours a day. Rod and line fishing did not exist but is a recent sport with more leisure time. The River Wharfe is a fair indication of this type of path which has been used for centuries. Proving this is often fairly easy, looking up the Enclosure Awards, where old pathways were delineated and maintained as access routes through the newly walled fields of big estates. A search of county archives where estate records are kept will reveal all; payments may also be found to gangs of men poling rafts or bow-hauling, thus proving that the river was used for navigation.

I was in Edinburgh when Clive Freshwater was taken to court by a Scottish estate, for insisting on his right to canoe the Spey. The defence was largely based on the fact that the river was used for logging at one period, and it was a matter of proving access points, where the logs could be rolled into the river to be later gathered downstream. After many days of hearing, the river was proved to be a public highway. The law appears to be based on the fact that once a highway, always a highway, even though the river has changed its character and is not now freely navigable by any means.

Often one is abused by fishermen standing on the banks of a public navigation. If you know your rights and you point this out to them, they simmer down rather quickly.

Fortunately, on the River Duddon, the area beyond the high tide limit was registered as a Common. The claimed registration was for the taking of shilla - small stones - which in this locality is used for making mortar for building by local residents. The eventual registration of this particular area was for "lawful recreation" as it had been used as a bathing area for many years. Mr. Peter "Angler" purchased the fishing rights for many thousands of pounds and erected barbed wire fences with notices prohibiting bathing and canoeing. The local paper was persuaded to take an interest in the dispute and Mr. "Angler" and his friends withdrew.

In most areas the erection of such notices on the river bank where the public have free access as "Private, no bathing, no boating" immediately suggests that there was once unrestricted use of the facilities referred to on the notices, and these notices should not go unchallenged.

Chapter 9
Sea Canoeing

It is said that there are grades of rivers up to six and then there is the sea. This has but one boundary, the shore, and presents the greatest hazard with its rocky, undertows, tides and currents.

Canoe Surfing

The canoeist must first find a storm beach with gently shelving sand; bays are best avoided as strong currents or tide rips occur at the edge of bays. With an on-shore wind producing waves about a foot high, paddle out to the break line, present your boat broadside-on to the waves, and with a low paddle brace into the wave, leaning vigorously seawards; the wave will pick up the boat and with a fight will carry the canoeist ashore - great fun!

LOW BRACE

Now try to gain more control. Paddle out to the break line, and low-brace into the wave with the paddle presented towards the bow of the canoe. This will turn the canoe into the wave, and the ride will continue with the canoeist now facing seawards. Move the blade towards the rear of the canoe and the boat will swing to face shorewards. A little more control can be gained by angling the paddle to make a stern rudder. Sooner or later you will be caught off balance and hammered into the beach - a friend standing by helps with the recovery of your equipment.

With increasing skill, bigger waves can be attempted, now using

STERN RUDDER

a high brace into the waves. With high braces and stern rudders a quick reaction and a delicate balance are required as the canoe weaves from side to side. A crowded beach is obviously not the place to be, so keep away from all bathers. If you are canoeing in company, as you pick up a wave shout, "My wave!", so that a clash of canoes is avoided. Many capsizes will occur. Go for the roll position with the paddle laid on the fore-deck, and the power of the wave will roll the canoeist up.

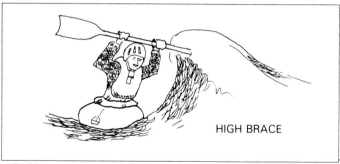

HIGH BRACE

On big waves, controlling your position is very important. If you drive forward, the bow will sink into the hollow of the wave, and the wave driving on will cause the canoe to loop. Looping if done deliberately can be great fun, but the first accidental loop is a shattering experience, especially if done in shallow water where the bow hits the sand and a pop-up occurs.

Beyond the break line lie the green-backed waves. These can be surfed with rather more control and help the canoeist on a coastal trip on his way.

Surfing a greenback. Photo: Brian Mitchinson

Beware of 'dumping waves' on a steep beach, where tons of water dump the canoeist onto the shingle with a strong undertow. Damage to both the canoeist and his equipment will result.

Sea Trips

When you have mastered the technique of coming ashore, the next headland beckons and a coastal trip results. While surfing, the canoeist will have noticed a 'long shore drift', which is influenced by the wind and tide. This must be taken into account if a return trip is contemplated, for an easy paddle out can result in a struggle on the return.

Using the help of the green-backed waves, one can surf down a wave until overtaken by it. Then you are left to flounder in the hollow with the difficulties of maintaining direction before being propelled forward by the next roller. The headland or the objective must always be in sight, or a complete loss of direction will result in the turmoil of the waves. The return trip is better undertaken in the lee of the shore, where there is some protection from the wind and the white-capped waves have lost some of their momentum. Beware when paddling in shallow water that there is a noticeable 'drag' from the water passing under the boat from your forward propulsion and the sea-bed below.

Canoeists in slalom boats have made extended sea trips, and it has been known for some to miss their destination because they have relied on eye-ball navigation. Sea trips must be planned affairs. A special canoe is required, a sea canoe. A sea canoe cuts through the waves and helps directional stability; a rudder will compensate for long shore drift or an unhelpful wind. Waterproof bulkheads will prevent a flooded boat, with the instability that results.

An essential item is a tide-table, for to paddle hard against a six-knot tide equals no progress at all; better to wait until the tide is in your favour and paddle with the tide. On the water a 'transit' will give you some idea of your progress. Note two features on the land (a lighthouse and a cottage, for example) and watch the apparent movement of the nearer object against the more distant. The time taken to 'close' the two features will give you some idea of your speed.

Taking a Fix

The Eskimo fixed a small table on the front of the cockpit, and on this he carried his fishing equipment. Today's canoeist on a long-distance trip requires something similar on which to keep his compass, pencil, scales, map and charts. In mist, which can develop suddenly, to know your position on the map is imperative.

To take a 'fix' requires the use of a compass of the 'Silva' type, on which it is possible to take a bearing off, say, a lighthouse (remember to subtract magnetic deviation shown on the margin of the map). A line can then be drawn on the map from the symbol representing the lighthouse on which the sighting was taken, and it is known that you are on that line. A cross-bearing is required at about right-angles to the first bearing, from another feature whose symbol is shown on the map. The second line is then drawn, and the cross represents your position. As a check, a third bearing could be taken, and the line drawn will produce a triangle. This is known as a 'cocked hat', and your position is within the triangle. A compass bearing is now taken to show your proposed direction. In poor light a canoeist paddling in front at the limit of visibility can be corrected left or right and the heading can be maintained.

Spare Equipment

This must not be carried in the cockpit area but must be stowed below hatches in the front or stern of the boat. A safe party is a minimum of three, all practised in the art of self-rescue. A whistle and flares should be carried by each member of the party, as well as first-aid kit and repair materials for the boat. A spare paddle can be stowed on the deck of one member's canoe. Emergency rations of a sustaining nature can help one out of trouble.

On an extended trip in open water, phone the coastguard to notify your destination and times of departure and arrival, and - most important - inform them when you have arrived. The party must stay together in case of any difficulty. Rain and wind will affect your progress and both can change dramatically without warning. Be aware that an off-shore wind can blow the sea flat and an on-shore wind will produce waves. Paddling against the wind will give short breaking waves; tide with wind will give long waves which can mean rapid progress, as the canoe can be surfed down the rollers.

Progress in open water can only be observed by taking transits. To try to paddle against the tide will mean no progress at all; the only course is to land and wait for the tide to turn. And remember that effort plus chill equals exposure.

In estuaries, as the tide runs out large areas of mud and sand are exposed. Try to follow the main channel, but you may often find false leads which can leave you stranded. Attempts to pull the canoe ashore may leave you floundering in mud or quicksand; better to wait until the tide returns.

This book starts at novice level, and it will take years of experience to attain standards of efficiency to master all types of water. Courses are available from the Sports Councils of England, Wales and Scotland. Take every opportunity of developing your skills. To canoe into the sunset and pull up on the silver strand, contented after a hard day's paddle, is an experience of a lifetime.

Appendix I
Terminology

Access Agreements
Negotiated use of rivers at cetrtain times

B.C.U.
British Canoe Union. The national governing body of canoeists in England

Boil
Water rising to the surface below a fall, containing large volume of air.

Buoyancy
Foamed material with large volume of air space, to keep boat or canoeist afloat

Bow
Front end of a boat

Bow Rudder
A steering stroke made at the bow

Chute
Main stream of a river running through a boulder choke

Coaming
Lip round the cockpit area

Cushion
Water piling up in front of a boulder

C1, C2
Canadian canoes used for slalom, single or double

Deep-water rescue
Method of righting capsized canoes, by other members of the party

Deck lines
Lines stretched from bow to stern, useful in open water

Eddy
Current diverging from the main stream

Feather
The two blades of a paddle are set at an angle to each other, either left or right

Ferry Glide
Using the power of the water flow to propel the boat across the river

Gunwhales
The top edge of the hull, where it meets the deck

Grading
Rivers are graded from 1 to 6 in order of difficulty

Haystacks
Standing waves in fast water, usually caused by boulders on the river bed

Heavy Water
Powerful river on rapid section

High Cross
Method of crossing fast-flowing river

J-stroke
Paddle stroke used to propel and steer Canadian canoes without lifting the single blade out of the water

Kayak
Eskimo canoe, decked in except for cockpit area

K1, K2
Racing kayaks, single and double, steered by rudder

Loop
Burying the bow of the canoe deep in the water and leaning forwards causes the stern to rise to a vertical position and fall

stern over bow

Main stream
Deepest channel of the river

Navigation
Rivers used in the past or the present for transport of goods by water

Pawlata
Roll using the paddle as a long lever. Named after an Austrian

Put Across
An early method of canoe rolling

Push Over
An overside canoe stroke to push the canoe away from obstacles

Raft
A number of canoes braced together alongside each other

Rocker
Curved keel, enabling boat to rock on its own length and spin on a vertical axis

Sill
Lip of a weir over which the water flows

Stern
Back end of the boat

Stopper
A wave rolling upstream, formed at the bottom of a weir or chute. Technically known as a hydraulic jump

Steyr Roll
Roll in a lay-back position

Spray Deck
Covering for cockpit area. Must be firm to resist the pressure of water

Screw Roll
Roll with the paddle held in normal position, using the paddle as a short lever

Storm Roll
Roll with a vertical paddle, used in aerated water which gives no purchase on the surface

Support Stroke
To prevent a capsize, could well be half a roll

Tail
Fast water below a rapid

Telemark
A method of turning the canoe

Toggle
Hand-grip on bow and stern

Appendix II
Useful Addresses

British Canoe Union,
Mapperley Hall,
Lucknow Avenue,
Nottingham. NG3 5FA
0602 691944

Scottish Canoe Association,
Caledonia House,
South Gyle,
Edinburgh. EH2 9QD

Welsh Canoe Association,
Pen y Bont,
Corwen,
Clwyd. Ll21 0EL

Instruction for all levels can be had at:-

Plas y Brenin National Centre,
Capel Curig,
Gwynedd. Ll24 0ET

Scottish National Centre,
Glenmore Lodge,
Glenmore,
Aviemore

Many other centres provide instruction

Canoe Focus is the official magazine of the British Canoe Union.

Flexel House,
45, High Street,
Addlestone,
Surrey. KT15 1TU

Books
Canoeing - Brailsford and Baker

Canoeing - The American National Red Cross

Slalom Canoeing - An introduction. B.C.U.

The Path of the Paddle - Bill Mason

Sea Canoeing - D.Hutchinson

Sea Kayaking - B.C.U. Symposium

Coastwise Navigation - Gordon

Canoeing down Everest - Mike Jones

Hypothermia, Frost-bite and
other cold injuries - B.C.U.

Living Canoeing - Alan Byde

Rivers of Cumbria - Mike Hay-
ward

Snowdonia White Water, Sea
and Surf - Terry Storry

*Many of the above are available
from the B.C.U. who also have:*

Scottish White Water Guide

Lake District White Water
Guide

River Severn Map

Canoeist Guide to the River
Wye

Guide to the rivers of the West
Midlands

Austrian and Bavarian river
guide

Alpine White Water guide

Canoeists map of French rivers

River Dordogne - French text

CICERONE PRESS BOOKS

Cicerone publish a range of guides to walking and climbing in
Britain and other general interest books

LAKE DISTRICT
LAKELAND VILLAGES
WORDSWORTH'S DUDDON REVISITED
REFLECTIONS ON THE LAKES
THE WESTMORLAND HERITAGE WALK
THE HIGH FELLS OF LAKELAND
IN SEARCH OF WESTMORLAND
CONISTON COPPER MINES - A Field Guide
CONISTER COPPER - A History
SCRAMBLES IN THE LAKE DISTRICT
WINTER CLIMBS IN THE LAKE DISTRICT
THE REGATTA MEN
LAKELAND - A Taste to Remember. (Recipes)
THE CHRONICLES OF MILNTHORPE
WALKS IN SILVERDALE/ARNSIDE - Area of
Outstanding Natural Beauty
BIRDS OF MORECAMBE BAY
THE EDEN WAY - OUR CUMBRIA
PETTIE (Memories of a Victorian Nursery)

NORTHERN ENGLAND
THE YORKSHIRE DALES
LAUGHS ALONG THE PENNINE WAY
(Cartoons)
THE RIBBLE WAY
NORTH YORK MOORS
WALKING THE CLEVELAND WAY AND
MISSING LINK
WALKS ON THE WEST PENNINE MOORS
WALKING NORTHERN RAILWAYS -
Vol.1. East Vol.2. West
BIRDS OF MERSEYSIDE
ROCK CLIMBS IN LANCASHIRE AND THE
NORTH WEST
THE ISLE OF MAN COASTAL PATH
HERITAGE TRAILS IN NORTH WEST
ENGLAND

DERBYSHIRE PEAK DISTRICT
WHITE PEAK WALKS Vol. 1 & 2
HIGH PEAK WALKS
WHITE PEAK WAY
KINDER LOG

WALES
THE RIDGES OF SNOWDONIA
HILL WALKING IN SNOWDONIA
ASCENT OF SNOWDON
WELSH WINTER CLIMBS
MOUNTAIN SUMMITS OF WALES
SNOWDONIA , WHITE WATER, SEA & SURF

WELSH BORDER
ROCK CLIMBS IN THE WEST MIDLANDS

SOUTH & WEST ENGLAND
WALKS IN KENT
THE WEALDWAY & VANGUARD WAY
THE SOUTH DOWNS WAY & DOWNS LINK
WALKING ON DARTMOOR
SOUTH WEST WAY - Vol. 1 & 2

SCOTLAND
SCRAMBLES IN LOCHABER
SCRAMBLES IN SKYE
ROCK CLIMBS: GLEN NEVIS & LOCHABER
OUTCROPS
THE ISLAND OF RHUM
CAIRNGORMS, WINTER CLIMBS
WINTER CLIMBS BEN NEVIS & GLENCOE
SCOTTISH RAILWAY WALKS

*Also a full range of guide-
books to walking, scrambling,
ice-climbing, rock climbing,
and other adventurous
pursuits in Britain and abroad.*

---

*Available from bookshops, outdoor equipment shops or direct (send
for price list) from: CICERONE PRESS, 2 POLICE SQUARE,
MILNTHORPE, CUMBRIA LA7 7PY*

CICERONE PRESS GUIDES

Cicerone publish a range of reliable guides to walking and climbing in Europe

FRANCE
TOUR OF MONT BLANC
CHAMONIX MONT BLANC - A Walking Guide
TOUR OF THE OISANS: GR54
WALKING THE FRENCH ALPS: GR5
THE CORSICAN HIGH LEVEL ROUTE: GR20
ROCK CLIMBS IN THE VERDON
THE WAY OF ST. JAMES: GR65

FRANCE/SPAIN
WALKS & CLIMBS IN THE PYRENEES

SPAIN
WALKING IN MALLORCA
WALKS & CLIMBS IN THE PICOS DE EUROPA

FRANCE/SWITZERLAND
THE JURA - Walking the High Route and Winter Ski Traverses

SWITZERLAND
WALKS IN THE ENGADINE
THE VALAIS - A Walking Guide

GERMANY/AUSTRIA
THE KALKALPEN TRAVERSE
KLETTERSTEIG - Scrambles in the Northern Limestone Alps
MOUNTAIN WALKING IN AUSTRIA
WALKING IN THE SALZKAMMERGUT
KING LUDWIG WAY

ITALY
ALTA VIA - High Level Walks in the Dolomites
VIA FERRATA - Scrambles in the Dolomites
ITALIAN ROCK - Selected Rock Climbs in Northern Italy
CLASSIC CLIMBS IN THE DOLOMITES

OTHER AREAS
THE MOUNTAINS OF GREECE - A Walker's Guide
TREKS & CLIMBS in the mountains of Rhum and Petra, JORDAN
CRETE: OFF THE BEATEN TRACK
ATLAS MOUNTAINS

GENERAL OUTDOOR BOOKS
LANDSCAPE PHOTOGRAPHY
FIRST AID FOR HILLWALKERS
MOUNTAIN WEATHER
JOURNEY AFTER DAWN
MOUNTAINEERING LITERATURE
SKI THE NORDIC WAY- A Manual of Cross-Country Skiing
THE ADVENTURE ALTERNATIVE

CANOEING
SNOWDONIA WILD WATER, SEA & SURF
WILDWATER CANOEING

CARTOON BOOKS
ON FOOT & FINGER
ON MORE FEET & FINGERS
LAUGHS ALONG THE PENNINE WAY

CICERONE PRESS

Also a full range of guide-books to walking, scrambling, ice-climbing, rock climbing, and other adventurous pursuits in Britain and abroad.

Other guides are constantly being added to the Cicerone List. Available from bookshops, outdoor equipment shops of direct (send for price list) from CICERONE PRESS, 2 POLICE SQUARE, MILNTHORPE CUMBRIA LA7 7PY

*Printed by Carnmor Print and Design
95/97 London Road, Preston, Lancashire*